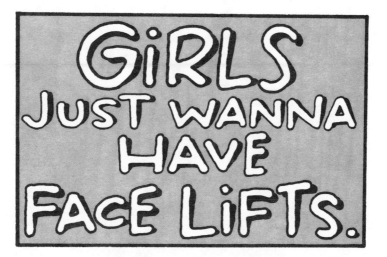

DESIGNED BY
ROB SCOTT AND MIKE WILLARD.

Published in the United States of America
by Hallmark Cards, Inc.

ISBN: 0-87529-638-6

Printed in the United States of America.

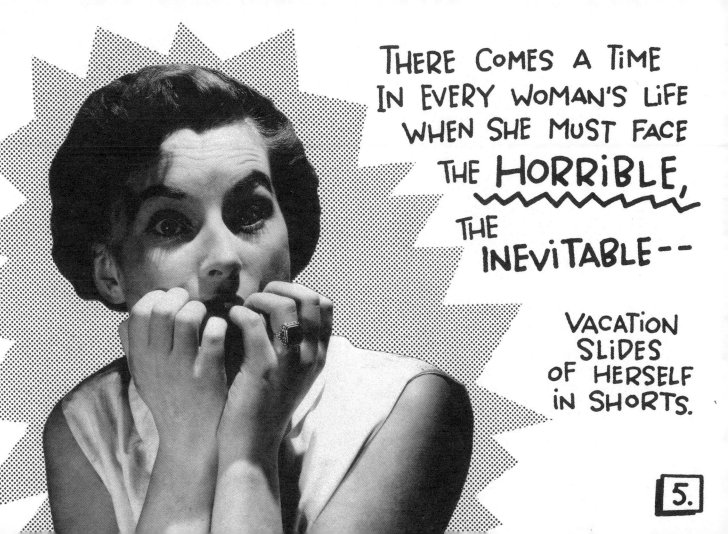

MAINTAINING A YOUTHFUL APPEARANCE REQUIRES ONLY A FEW THINGS:

REST,   EXERCISE,   A BALANCED DIET,

AND A COSMETIC SURGERY BUDGET EQUAL TO THE NATIONAL DEBT.

7.

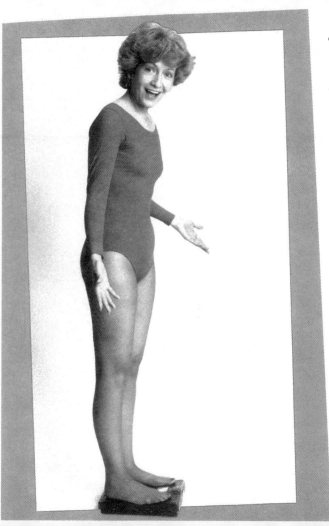

To Avoid Putting on Unwanted Pounds, There Are Only TWO Things You Need to Avoid--

Food and Drink.

9.

IT IS RECOMMENDED THAT EVERY WOMAN SPEND AN HOUR A DAY ENGAGED IN STRENUOUS ACTIVITY...
UNFORTUNATELY, THERE ISN'T ALWAYS ENOUGH GOSSIP TO LAST AN HOUR.
11.

AEROBICS CLASSES OFFER MANY OPPORTUNITIES FOR HEALTHY EXERCISE:

STRETCHING, TONING, STRANGLING THE PERKY SIZE 3 INSTRUCTOR.

15.

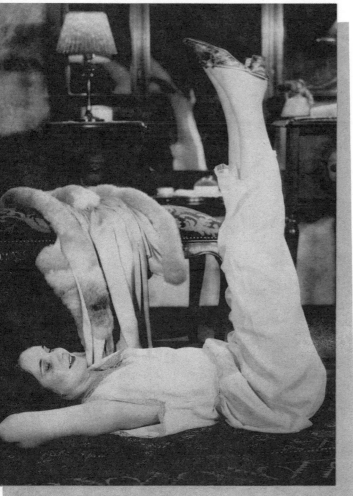

HAVING THE PERFECT BODY ISN'T DIFFICULT...

IT'S IMPOSSIBLE!

17.

HERE'S A LiTTLE MAKE-UP TiP FROM ONE OF HOLLYWOOD'S TOP MAKE-UP ARTiSTS--

USE LOTS.

19.

YOU KNOW
YOU'RE
GETTING
OLDER
〰〰
WHEN
THEY ASK
TO CHECK
YOUR BAGS
AND YOU
AREN'T CARRYING
ANY LUGGAGE.

21.

REMEMBER THESE TWO SIMPLE STEPS TO ENHANCE YOUR APPEARANCE:

 BUY AN EXPENSIVE FULL-LENGTH COAT.

 NEVER, EVER TAKE IT OFF.

23.

25.

WITH AGE
A WOMAN GAINS
WISDOM,
MATURITY,
SELF-
ASSURANCE

AND TEN POUNDS
RIGHT ON THE HIPS.

IT'S <u>EASY</u> TO FIT INTO THE CLOTHES YOU WORE IN

HIGH SCHOOL...

PROVIDED YOU WERE EXTREMELY FAT IN HIGH SCHOOL.

29.

DON'T WORRY-

MANY MEN STILL FIND OLDER WOMEN ATTRACTIVE...

OLD, STOOPED-OVER MEN WHO TALK TO WASTEBASKETS, THAT IS.

33.

YOU'RE AT THE AGE WHEN YOU CAN APPRECIATE THE

FINER THINGS IN LIFE--

YOU CAN'T DO ANY OF 'EM... BUT YOU CAN APPRECIATE THEM.

37.

THERE ARE WORSE THINGS THAN GETTING OLDER··

YOU COULD PUT YOUR TEETH IN BACKWARDS AND GIVE YOURSELF A TONSILLECTOMY.

39.

BRAVE

IS THE WOMAN WHO DARES TO DREAM AN IMPOSSIBLE DREAM,

FACE A NEW CHALLENGE...

...TRY ON A TWO-PIECE SWIMSUIT.

41.

MAKE **LAUGHTER** A PART OF EVERY DAY...

LOOK AT YOURSELF NAKED IN THE MIRROR.

43.

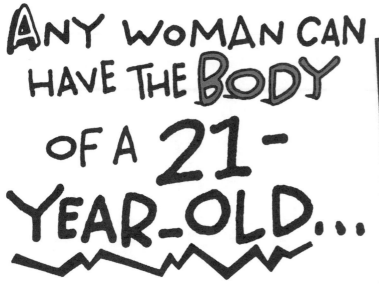

ANY WOMAN CAN HAVE THE *BODY* OF A 21-YEAR-OLD...

AS LONG AS SHE BUYS HIM A FEW DRINKS FIRST.

45.

EVERY WOMAN
INSTINCTIVELY
KNOWS
THAT ONE SPECIAL
WAY TO DRIVE A
MAN WILD...

HIDE THE T.V.
REMOTE CONTROL.

YOU KNOW YOU'RE GETTING UP THERE WHEN YOU BOB FOR APPLES BECAUSE THEY'RE A GOOD SOURCE OF FIBER.

49.

LIKE GOOD WINE, WE GROW MORE MELLOW WITH AGE, AND, AS WE AGE, WE GROW MORE MELLOW WITH WINE.

53.

LIFE STILL OFFERS FUN AND EXCITEMENT WHEN YOU'RE OLD...

IT JUST OFFERS THEM TO YOUNGER PEOPLE.

55.

A SUCCESSFUL CAREER CAN

BRING FULFILLMENT, SECURITY, INDEPENDENCE AND MOST IMPORTANTLY--

AN OPPORTUNITY TO OGLE THE YOUNG GUYS IN THE MAILROOM.

CHARACTER IS BUILT BY OVERCOMING LIFE'S TRAGEDIES--
A SHATTERED DREAM, A BITTER DISAPPOINTMENT, AND WORST OF ALL...

A BAD DYE JOB.

59.

AS YOU GET OLDER, YOU CAN STILL TAKE :PRIDE: IN YOUR ACCOMPLISHMENTS--

LIKE STAYING AWAKE FOR AN ENTIRE RENTED MOVIE.

61.

DON'T LET THE CHANGE OF LIFE GET YOU

DOWN...

IT'S SO HARD
TO GET BACK UP.